HER Thoughts

Soyo Lane

BookLeaf
Publishing

India | USA | UK

Presentation by *BookLeaf Publishing*

Web: www.bookleafpub.com

E-mail: info@bookleafpub.com

ISBN: 9789358315073

First edition 2023

DEDICATION

This book is dedicated to all those who understand there is a special power in expressing your feelings. We don't all have the courage to speak our truth, but I hope this book finds YOU and encourages YOU to do just that......YOU are worth being heard.

ACKNOWLEDGEMENT

Thank you lord. You hear me when no one else is listening.

To my dad to whom I attribute my open and raw thoughts and opinions. He valued my opinion at a young age and made me feel comfortable enough to express myself no matter when to whom and about what. To my mother, from whom this natural gift was conceptualized. To my husband, to whom half my life was experienced....I know you were waiting on your diss track, not this time! To my babies, Yari, Amari and Cali, you are my motivation!! To my siblings, I hope I have made you proud and filled the shoes of big sister!

My friends and family who have poured into me throughout the years, I love you. Thank you for listening to me vent, cry and celebrate.

This is just the beginning!!!

Entitled Ole Me

I'm entitled to be respected.
To which is given can be taken.
I'm entitled to receive love as deep as I give it.
I'm entitled to my opinion, even if it differs from
yours.
I'm entitled to express myself
behind the confides of closed doors.
I'm entitled to have biases that shape my
thinking.
I'm entitled to elevate my mind
to minimize the effects of it shrinking.
I'm entitled to expand my vocabulary
beyond the limited resources I've been given.

**You can believe in yourself and be deserving
of privileges without it demeaning others. Be
entitled.

Lip Service

Something about intellect.
It drives me wild.
It's passionate.
It's intriguing.
It's as explosive as a land mine.
You were born with a mouth, lips and a tongue
but if all you are making is noise
you have lots to learn.
The way you articulate your words
leave most in a state of awe.
The complexity, and the depth in you
at times can't be understood by you
The term sapiosexual is one that attracts beings
of your kind
But "they're just words" others say
How can that create a love line?
The feelings your words create
are more than phonemic expressions
they manifest,
they illustrate
They reflect a lingual blessing.

**Your mouth is a powerful tool…..use it
wisely!

Hidden Lines

Boundaries, Oh Boundaries where art thou???
I've looked high and I've looked low, but still
nowhere to be found. Please give me space. It's
not a personal thing, just protecting my peace. I
want to cry when no one is looking, and I don't
want to answer any questions. Leave me in my
feelings. My boundaries are mine and you don't
get to determine how, what or when. Despite the
line being invisible, it's still dark and loud. I
want to determine it sooner than later. MY
boundaries stand out in the middle of a crowd.
Others have expectations of what your
boundaries should contain, but those are the
same people who only look out for "they". The
feelings of empowerment that come with setting
the tone. Please give me my space. I just want to
be left alone.

Puffed Love

Say nothing and everything at the same damn
time....why must it always end up this way!
Sometimes being sick and tired of being sick
and tired is a crippling crutch....a gut-wrenching
feeling because there are things said that cannot
be taken back.
The anger derives from pain but when that pain
is lifelong and started before you and will end
after you there is no solution!
No matter what, you're wrong when you're right
and wrong when you're wrong. Why can't
things be so simple???
Because life's not, it's all about balance.
With the ups and downs come the fucked up in
between.
No one can read minds and if you read mine I
would probably be fined!
I can't understand why you don't understand???
There's no place for puffed, displaced love.
Love is kind...love doesn't give up.
If you truly live life on a frequency of love, a
high vibration you will attract such beings.
If you continue the other route you will become
that and that's not a place to lie.

Lay with dogs you'll wake up with fleas!!!
Eagles soar with eagles not ducks!!!
Peace ✌

**A puffed chest makes for a weak heart. Love shouldn't bring endless hurt. A healing heart is an understanding heart.

Anxious eyes

Wide and alert
Jitters and fears
Why are things so blurry
I really hate it here
No one's looking
and my heart is pounding out loud
Eyes wide shut
I feel alone in this crowd
Anxious eyes please let me sleep
I have things to do tomorrow
Anxious eyes don't care about sleep
They hope the worry will follow.

**I wish peace to all the people who feel my pain. Anxiety is no joke. It's way too random to contain when your worries are getting the best of you in the middle of the night. Understand that I understand you and just try and close those damn anxious eyes.

Talk to me nice

I speak with my heart.
So my emotions are pure
Tears flowing, voices raised
My passion can be mistaken for rage.
My heart is normally worn on my sleeve
But the same way it beeps
Is the same way my tone
changes when I speak.
Monotone-nope
Disingenuous-never
Always true to self
Authentic and clever.
These conversations end with closure,
begins with the happily ever after's

The passion in my soul won't allow me to
remain bottled,
If I get to going it's all talk
without time to breathe or swallow.
I love hard but can be hard to love.
Bring the intensity,
I'll match it with vigor,
Perspective is key,
Very misunderstood,
Go figure........

10/24/2018

Shit went bad fast
Felt like there was no way out
Walls closing in faster and faster
Someone please help with this doubt
When you look down
And downs looking up
You know your time is coming
So just stay prayed up
When the calls are coming slow
And the text messages are almost obsolete
The lord said he wouldn't put more on me than I
can bear
Lord I promise
I believe
The strength of an ox
The tenacity of ten men
I know "this" won't last but can this shit end

**This is literally how I felt on this day. The message in it all is I was going through a battle that I felt was never-ending. Five years later I have no idea what I was battling…..nothing lasts forever. Hard times make you feel that way but we can get through it🩶

Father, Dad and Man

You were a part of the first
and will forever be the last.
Man, how could you be the entire definition of
Father, Dad and Man?
When the world said, "No never" and you said
"Watch and see"
Dad, I know you are flawed
But, father you are everything to me.
Man, you speak words of wisdom,
history, street and truth.
There will never ever be a man who can fill
those shoes
you speak to us in a language
that few can truly understand,
What does "Rule # 2 and Rule #17"
mean to the average human?
Father figure you will always be
to us, them, and the world
They say It takes a village to raise a child
Well damn, how much of the village rent did you
afford????

You always put us first
before woman, work and the world
The repayment is a forever debt

How can one man know everything about anything?
I tried to test you and see.
But damn, I asked you about a car engine two hours later I was an expert in anthropology!

**Dedicated to a real one!!! Daddy issues are real. But when you are raised with a real one it's a true blessing! We get the best of both worlds. I don't fit your mold world but I know someone who loves me unconditionally, with flaws and all!!! It doesn't have to be biological either y'all…..daddy love comes from the soul, not the blood♥

Here and Now

It's more than a song
It's a way of life
You're here and I want you now
Without the painful stressful plight
You're here and I want you now
Please don't talk. Just listen

You're here and I want now
Leave all the trauma and ego behind you
You're here and I want you now
What does it take for you just to unwind?
Please come here because I want you now
Just read between the lines
I know you are not here but I still want you
know
Make it happen baby,
This is not how the story ends
I am here and you are here now
Things worked out all we had to do was say it
out loud.

**Here and now. You can be in the same room with someone and be mentally miles away. You're here and I want you know is a reminder to be in the present, near and far. We want who and what we want. Be here with me because I want you now. Physically and Mentally.

Mouth Moves

Mouth moves hinder you
They steal your joy like a thief in the night
Mouth moves weigh you down
The fear it creates is a severe case of fight or
flight
The expectation we set for ourselves
Takes perseverance and a little ability
But when those mouth moves are in motion
You set an unrealistic form of accountability
It's okay to move in silence
And let your work proceed your voice
But the longing for others' opinions of you
Is unhealthy but mouth moves have no choice
They move loud and proud
And rarely have it to show
Those mouth moves can lead a parade
And be the only joker on the float.

**Silence is golden.
And in times of show and tell a very rare occurrence. It is okay to make plans and create without a crowd. Too many times we let "them" in and they're silently working against you. And we wonder why some of our ideas never see fruition.

Sweet Dreams

As I lay here counting these sheep
I am trying to get close to you.
My eyelids are getting heavy,
But they're refusing closure.
I wake up in a cold sweat,
but can't remember your face.
My heart is pounding out of my chest,
like I just ran a race.
I can't wait until we meet again,
The anticipation is killing me.
I need this feeling inside of me,
It's just getting harder to remember it.
There's always a sense of urgency,
Always sneaking and hiding.
I think about you all through the day,
Can't wait to get undressed in hopes you'll
Soon come and find me.
Oh my sweet dreams,
You replenish me like no other.
Thank you, bed, for my sweet dreams
All I need now is a few hours and some warm
covers.

The Happiest Hour

Timing is always too short
But the memories last forever
Do you prefer?
Bubbly, sweet, or bland
Clear, brown or tan
Let's do 5 PM to seven or maybe 8 PM to close
It's a girls' night or a game time
The occasion doesn't matter
Let's just go
Spinach dip or chicken wings
Salad or a slider
Let your hair down
Be merry and free
But be on time
Those 1/2 price menu options are key

Everyone loves a little happy hour. No expectations, just a little unwind time for the working folks. This poem is that……just some fun when shit gets too deep🩶

Those Nonverbals

It's the things we don't say
That speak the loudest and clearest
It's the kinetics mixed with the posture I can see
on the other side of the sphere.
When you look at me like that
and your forehead crinkles up
even when you say "you're good" that
paralanguage says enough

Chronemics is a new cue for me but it's getting
easier to follow.
The timing means everything
So let's table this conversation and long pauses
help with building
the anticipation.

Proximity is the end of me
please take a step back.
I don't think we have to say another word
you're too close and about to get smacked.

***You can say a lot while saying nothing at all.
Those nonverbal cues are powerful.

Sight and sounds of peace

Can you see the light?
The storm is slowing ahead
The crashing sounds of waves
Magnifying calming wind to the ears
The sight is surreal
The tunnels of light are magical
The thoughts of peace mixed with the sounds of
love
Bring moments of clarity
It's like being ambushed by nature
A true beauty description
Higher vibrations
Cloud like beings
No better place than this

**Moving to the desert gives you a different love and appreciation for God's simple treasure.....like the ocean. That place does wonders for your mental health and sanity!!! We took the proximity for granted. The sight and sound of the ocean is peace.

Auspicious

Are you living a purpose-driven life?
Are you constantly in a state of
"Gotta get it right"?
When you look in the mirror
do you smile?
Is your lens focusing clearer?
Are your goals appearing nearer now?
When you talk, do they listen?
Is your skin magically glistening?
Do you feel the "feels" inside out?
Can you combat the criticism
That spews from "their" mouths?
Timing is key.
And it's happening now.

Your aura is a strong magnetic field.
Your chakras are aligned.
If you can't resonate with these thoughts,
Just wait...
It's only a matter of time.

Methuselah Tree

Pain, hurt, frustration.
Anger, terror and fear.
Strength, perseverance, patience.
Love, pride and cheers.

We've been burnt, struck and hung.
Whipped, shot and killed.

The story is never ending,
Like the branches on this tree.

The years of our hurt
The struggles of our past
Yet today we still are on a mirrored path.

Do we see the light?
Is it shining through?
Is the tunnel clear?
Are we free?

False imagery, lies and deceit.
Are we sure we've got to a place of equality?

These slanted eyes

These slanted eyes are mysterious
These slanted eyes are clear
These slanted eyes are my navigation system
through life
These slanted eyes show my deepest fears

These slanted eyes have seen the worse
These slanted eyes have cried many tears
These slanted eyes are the keys to my soul
These slanted eyes are sincere

These slanted eyes assist in my discernment
These slanted eyes guide my heart
These slanted eyes can see right through you
These slanted eyes tell what my mouth cannot

These slanted eyes hold nothing back
These slanted eyes will love you forever
These slanted eyes will never forsake you
These slanted eyes hold my dearest treasures

Fear

I can't
It won't happen
Maybe later
Struggles
Empty promises
Failure
Seeking validation
Can't seem to find it
Self sabotage
Timidity
Loss cause
Never trying
Tons of excuses
Looking for the next chance
Anxiety
Panic
Habituating feelings
Circumstance

**The fear of failure has been a barrier for me and lots of my endeavors. I am trying to overcome my obsession with procrastination and take more leaps, get out of my own way🩶

Intuition

I know it's there.
I just cannot seem to find it
This feeling won't leave me
I've tried but I cannot hide it
These emotions are getting stronger
But the conscious reasoning isn't there
The air between us is getting thicker
I know something's up but
I can't pull it from thin air
My intuitive conviction tells me different
than the information provided
These thoughts are not random occurrences.
there is some truth behind them
Never go against your intuition because it's only
a matter of time
But don't linger in the intuitive space too long
What is meant to be will find you

Alignment

We're a unified front
An aligned coalition
Collaborating communication
Solidarity
Strong foundation

In a state of disarray
Constant conflict and
Confusion
Endless disfunction
With no resolution

An emotional entanglement
Filled with intimacy and passion
It's more than physical
it's a soul connection
We're a force to be reckoned with
When alignment is intact

Physical is minimal
Passive aggression is back
No common ground
The enemy is being let in
Understanding is at the backburner
Anger has sunk in.

24

**Can alignment and detachment coexist?

Fear Does not and Will not!

25

Fear does not and will not control me.
I won't let it stop me from being who I want to
be.
I won't let it take control.

I've been there before, and I don't want to go
back.
I won't stop doing what I'm doing just because I
lack.

CONTROL is what I have.
and with the powers vested in me.
I'll keep on as I please.
With no fear, discouragement or worries.

I'll continue to work hard,
with the power that I have.
I will not let fear make me sad!
Fear does not and will not control me.

Written by Cali Skye Lane*